Original title:
Jewelled Bits Over the Witch Hull

Author: Liisi Lendorav
ISBN HARDBACK: 978-1-80562-602-2
ISBN PAPERBACK: 978-1-80564-123-0

Silken Dreams in the Embrace of Shadows

In twilight's hush, where whispers creep,
A world of wonders starts to seep.
With silken threads, the night unfolds,
As secrets dance, and fate beholds.

Beneath the moon, a silver glow,
A pathway winds where dreamers go.
The stars cascade like fallen dew,
While sleep devours the waking view.

The shadows weave a tapestry,
Of memories, lost yet meant to be.
With each soft sigh, the darkness sighs,
And cradles hopes in lullabies.

In every corner, magic stirs,
With fleeting forms of fleeting birds.
A flicker here, a fluttered wing,
The night conceals what daylight brings.

So let your silken dreams take flight,
In woven realms of endless night.
Embrace the quiet, hold it tight,
For shadows bloom in fading light.

Spirals of Light in the Elderwood

Deep within the whispering trees,
Where ancient magic bends the breeze,
Light dances through the emerald leaves,
In spirals woven, the heart believes.

A flicker bright, a glowing trail,
Guides the lost through shadowed veil,
Each flicker tells a tale untold,
Of daring dreams and journeys bold.

The roots entwined in secrets deep,
Guard memories that softly weep,
For light reveals what darkness hides,
In the Elderwood, where hope abides.

With every step on mossy ground,
A melody of peace is found,
The spirals twirl, the spirits gleam,
In harmony, they weave the dream.

So venture forth where few have roamed,
In sacred woods, where light has combed,
With every whisper, truth ignites,
In spirals of light, the heart delights.

The Hidden Spark of Shadow's Edge

Beneath the veil where shadows blend,
A hidden spark awaits a friend,
In darkness lay the brightest flame,
A secret known without a name.

Whispers flicker, thoughts take flight,
In hidden corners, shrouded tight,
The spark awaits a daring soul,
To cast away the dark's control.

At shadow's edge, where dreams unfold,
The timid hearts grow brave and bold,
For in the dark, the truth resides,
With starlit paths as guides and guides.

Fear not the chill that lingers near,
For every dread can disappear,
With one small spark igniting bright,
To turn the shadows into light.

So heed the call of quiet night,
Unlock the door to hidden light,
And in that spark, your courage found,
To dance among the shadows' sound.

Artifacts of Twilight's Kiss

When twilight wraps the world in dreams,
And silken twilight softly gleams,
There lie the artifacts of old,
In whispers sweet, their tales unfold.

Each trinket holds a memory dear,
Of laughter shared and fleeting cheer,
Beneath the stars, with eyes that glow,
The treasures speak of long ago.

A pendant pure of silver spun,
Tells of the battle lost and won,
With every touch, a story sings,
Of magic wrought by fated things.

Cloaks of mist and crystal tears,
Bear witness to forgotten years,
In twilight's kiss, the past awakes,
As heartbeats stir and silence breaks.

So wander forth in evening's grace,
Where shining artifacts embrace,
And let their stories guide your way,
Through twilight's chill to brighter days.

Starry Tresses of a Sorceress's Web

In a realm where starlight weaves,
Through gossamer and silver leaves,
A sorceress spins her mystic threads,
With starry tresses upon her head.

Her whispers dance like summer air,
Each word a spell, a woven prayer,
With every strand, the night ignites,
As dreams take flight on velvet nights.

Through galaxies, her fingers glide,
Casting wonders far and wide,
In webs of light, her secrets twine,
A tapestry of pure design.

The moon, her muse, beams soft and clear,
While shadows gather, drawing near,
But in her gaze, the cosmos glows,
With every knot, the magic flows.

So seek the sorceress at dusk,
And feel the stardust's gentle husk,
In tresses woven, the heart shall find,
A universe of dreams aligned.

Prismatic Echoes of Serene Nightfall

Whispers weave through twilight's purple haze,
Beneath the stars, where silence softly plays.
Shadows dance on cobblestones of dreams,
In every heart, a flicker gently beams.

The moonlight spills like silver on the earth,
Lending the night a sense of quiet worth.
Veils of starlight drape the world in grace,
As every moment finds its sacred place.

With every breath, the cosmos sings anew,
Its symphony in colors deep and true.
Where time dissolves, and worries fade to dust,
In the embrace of night, we find our trust.

Echoes beckon from the realms unseen,
Where hope ignites the dark with vibrant sheen.
Each pulse of light, a promise to explore,
In prismatic dreams, we long to soar.

So linger here, where night's caress unfolds,
In vibrant tales that only silence holds.
For in this realm where shadows softly blend,
The echoes call us home, till night must end.

Secrets Laced in Enigmatic Grains

In the silence, secrets buried deep,
Whispers of time, where shadows softly creep.
Every grain of sand, a tale to tell,
Of magic woven in an ancient spell.

Beneath the surface, mysteries entwined,
A tapestry of thoughts that fate designed.
In the stillness, echoes of the past,
Each fleeting moment, a spellcast vast.

With every step upon the dusky shore,
The grains confide whatever lies in store.
Footprints linger, stories fade away,
Yet in their silence, legends still hold sway.

An evening breeze carries the unspoken,
In the twilight hour, no words are broken.
Secrets laced in shadows, gently spun,
An endless journey, where we all are one.

So close your eyes and feel the ancient rhyme,
Let secrets guide you, lost in space and time.
For within each grain, the universe entwines,
A dance of souls, where every heart defines.

Twinkling Charms Above the Hallowed Ground

Amidst the night, where dreams begin to wake,
Twinkling charms beam down, a path we make.
Underneath the heavens, stories glow,
In every twinkle lies a sacred flow.

Beneath the stars, the world beneath our feet,
Hallowed ground whispers secrets bittersweet.
Echoes of laughter ride the gentle breeze,
In this enchanted realm, our hearts find ease.

Each charm a wish, a hope that takes its flight,
Dancing with the shadows, embracing light.
Together we stand, in wonder's embrace,
As twinkling charms guide us to a new space.

So gather 'round, let your spirit soar high,
In the cosmic dance that lights the night sky.
For in these moments, with every heartbeat bound,
We find our way through the hallowed ground.

Let starlit magic sprinkle dreams above,
Inviting us to cherish all we love.
For in this twinkle, we find our true sound,
A symphony of life on sacred ground.

Iridescent Particles in the Midnight Swirl

In the midnight swirl, where colors collide,
Iridescent particles drift and glide.
Each fleeting spark, a story to unfold,
In the depths of night, where dreams are sold.

With every breath, the universe expands,
Twirling treasures slip through gentle hands.
A dance of light, a cosmic ballet spun,
In the fabric of night, we all are one.

Awash in hues, a canvas pure and bright,
Invisible threads weave us through the night.
As laughter twinkles through the veils of dark,
In the stillness, every heart leaves its mark.

So take a step into the wild unknown,
Let vibrant winds guide you, though you may roam.
In this midnight swirl, let your spirit sway,
For iridescent dreams will light the way.

In the quiet, listen to the song of stars,
Echoing tales from Jupiter to Mars.
In this grand adventure, together we'll whirl,
In iridescent joy of the midnight swirl.

The Crystal Silence of the Enchanted Night

In shadows deep, where secrets dwell,
The moonlight weaves its silken spell.
Stars shimmer bright, a guiding light,
In crystal silence, all feels right.

Whispers drift upon the breeze,
Dancing through the ancient trees.
Magic lingers, soft and sweet,
Where night and day in silence meet.

A silver glow on dewy grass,
Each twinkle hints of dreams to pass.
In twilight's charm, we find our way,
To realms where night can softly sway.

The world is hushed, a sacred pause,
With every breath, our hearts applause.
In enchanted night, we dare to roam,
Through crystal silence, we find home.

Moonlit Gems in the Hands of Time

Moonlit gems in hands so fine,
Whispers of fate in every line.
Moments trapped in glistening glass,
As shadows waltz and memories pass.

Ticking softly, the clock does chime,
Bottled dreams in the flow of time.
Each spark a tale from ages old,
Secrets twinkling, waiting to be told.

In the depths of night, we dare to gaze,
At time's embrace and its mystic plays.
In every heartbeat, a story we find,
As moonlit gems illuminate the mind.

With every tick, a choice to make,
The path ahead, our hearts awake.
Through silver beams, we craft our rhyme,
Forever linked in the hands of time.

Soft Whispers of the Starry Vines

Soft whispers breeze through leaves entwined,
Secrets shared in the night, so kind.
Starry vines reach high and low,
In gentle moonlight, magic flows.

Embrace the night, let worries fade,
In the dance of shadows, dreams are made.
A tapestry of light and sound,
Where hopes and passions twirl around.

With every sigh, the stars reply,
Casting wishes into the sky.
In vines of silver, our hearts conspire,
To chase the dreams we all desire.

Down hidden paths, where starlights play,
We wander softly, lose our way.
In whispered truths, we find our place,
Among the night's enchanting grace.

Echoes of Luminosity Amidst Twilight's Palette

Echoes of light in twilight's embrace,
Splashing colors on nature’s face.
Whirling hues that dance and swirl,
Painting moments in soft, bright pearls.

The sun dips low, a golden crown,
As shadows rise, their veil comes down.
A canvas stretched from dusk to dawn,
Where dreams awaken, and fears are drawn.

In every hue, a story found,
Of love and loss, of joy unbound.
With echoes soft, the heart takes flight,
In twilight's glow, all feels just right.

Through vivid whispers, the night does call,
Inviting each soul to heed its thrall.
In luminous shades, we find our song,
Echoes of beauty where hearts belong.

Mystical Jewels from the Fey Realm

In the woods where shadows play,
Sparkling gems in the light of day.
Whispers of magic in the trees,
Fey folk dancing on the breeze.

Crimson pearls and emerald green,
Glimmers bright, a wondrous scene.
Each jewel holds a tale untold,
Of ancient secrets, brave and bold.

Twinkling stars, the night's embrace,
Fey laughter echoes, a fanciful chase.
Boundless dreams in twilight's grace,
Mystical realms in a timeless space.

By moonlit paths, they softly tread,
A tapestry of wonder spread.
Hearts enchanted, lost in bliss,
In fey twilight, we find our wish.

The Enchantment of Glimmering Dusk

As daylight fades to softest sigh,
The sky transforms, a velvet dye.
Stars awaken, twinkling bright,
Drawing magic from the night.

Colors dance on the horizon's edge,
Promises whispered, a silent pledge.
Silhouettes cast in luminous glow,
Where dreams awaken, and spirits flow.

Moonbeams scatter like playful sprites,
Chasing shadows through autumn nights.
In this hour of shimmering light,
Hope ignites, a beacon bright.

With every breath, enchantment sings,
Nature stirs as dusk takes wings.
A tapestry woven of care and dreams,
In the quiet, the world redeems.

Fragments of the Sky’s Laughter

When clouds part ways, laughter spills,
Fragments of joy meet gentle hills.
Bright as sunshine, warming hearts,
Life's sweet treasures, joyful parts.

In every breeze, a chuckle clear,
Each fluttering leaf, a memory dear.
The sun's embrace, the sky's delight,
Whispers of wonders, day and night.

Raindrops fall like playful tears,
Glimmers of hope dancing through fears.
In puddles, reflections of dreams,
A symphony woven in sunlight beams.

Nature’s song, a timeless dance,
Laughter shared in sweet romance.
In every moment, the world aligns,
Fragments of laughter, love intertwines.

Ciphers of Light Within the Gloom

In shadowed corners, lost and found,
Ciphers of light upon the ground.
Hints of brilliance, faintly glow,
Guiding pathways through the woe.

A flicker bright in endless night,
Crackling shadows, whispers of light.
Hopes ignited in hidden grace,
Each soft shimmer a warm embrace.

Through tangled branches, secrets hide,
Tracing paths where dreams abide.
In the quiet, a voice calls clear,
Illuminating paths, drawing near.

As darkness wanes, the dawn does rise,
Glimmers weave through the waking skies.
Ciphers of hope through night's dismay,
Promising light, a brand new day.

Mystical Reflections on a Serpent's Tail

In twilight's grasp, the serpent coils,
With scales that gleam in silver oils.
Its eyes like stars, a secret keeps,
Through ancient woods, a magic creeps.

Beneath the moon, it twists and sways,
A dance of shadows, night to praise.
The whispers of the past arise,
In every scale, a tale lies.

As echoes of forgotten lore,
Entwine the heart with dreams of yore.
Through serpents' tales, the truth unfolds,
A mystery that never grows old.

With every flick of its long tail,
It beckons souls, where wonders hail.
In dreams, we wander, spirits bold,
Along the paths where tales are told.

So let us dive in twilight's sea,
Where magic swirls, and we are free.
With serpents' grace, we find our way,
In reflections, night gives sway.

Quartz and Ambrosia in a Sorceress's Grasp

In a glade where shadows play,
A sorceress weaves night and day.
With quartz that sparkles, wild and bright,
And ambrosia's kiss, she conjures light.

Her fingers dance with ancient runes,
As soft as whispers of forgotten tunes.
Each crystal hums a gentle tune,
Embracing dusk, inviting moon.

With every breath, potion she makes,
The universe bends, the essence wakes.
In her cauldron, stars ignite,
A tapestry of endless night.

Around her, nature holds its breath,
As magic pulses, life, and death.
With quartz and berries, dreams collide,
In sorcery's grace, we abide.

With a glance that sees beyond the veil,
She crafts the winds, she surges the gale.
In her realm of wonder, time suspends,
Quartz and ambrosia, the magic blends.

Shadows Glinting in Celestial Veils

In the night where shadows wend,
Celestial veils begin to blend.
Stars like jewels, they softly gleam,
Whispering secrets to the dream.

Each twinkle tells of worlds unknown,
Where echoes of the past have flown.
Through velvet skies, the shadows dance,
Painting tales of fate and chance.

With glimmers bright and hazy light,
They guide the lost through endless night.
A symphony of dark and bright,
A balance held in silent flight.

In cosmic realms where time does bend,
The shadows stir, their magic send.
Through every flicker, a promise grows,
Of hope that in the darkness glows.

So, gaze upon the endless sky,
Where shadows swim, and spirits sigh.
In celestial veils, we find our way,
Through glinting stars, forever stay.

Whispers of the Forest in Silken Threads

In a forest deep, where silence lies,
Whispers float like butterflies.
Among the trees with trunks so grand,
The secrets weave a silken strand.

Nature's breath, a gentle sigh,
Through leaves that dance, they flutter by.
Each thread of sound, a story spins,
Of ancient spirits, lost in winds.

The brook hums soft, a lullaby,
As fireflies blink like stars on high.
With every step, the echoes call,
A magic woven, binding all.

In mossy beds and ferns so bright,
The whispers linger, pure delight.
With every heartbeat, nature thrives,
In silken threads, the forest lives.

So wander deep, where shadows roam,
Through whispered words, make it your home.
In the forest’s arms, forever stay,
Where silken threads shall guide your way.

Charmed Shards in the Twilight's Embrace

In twilight's hush, the whispers call,
Where secrets dance and shadows fall.
A flicker glows through trees entwined,
As magic sparks, the heart aligned.

With every step, the stars descend,
Embraced by night, as dreams suspend.
Each shard of light a story weaves,
In twilight's arms, the soul believes.

The moonlight bathes the earth in grace,
While echoes of the past embrace.
Through tangled roots and glowing streams,
Awake within the creatures' dreams.

A gentle sigh of evening air,
Invokes the magic lingering there.
With open heart, the journey starts,
In charmed shards, we find our parts.

Radiant Echoes of a Bewitched Realm

In realms where magic softly gleams,
The echoes weave enchanting dreams.
With every breath, a spell is spun,
Beneath the gaze of the watching sun.

Through velvet nights, the starlit skies,
Reveal the truth in whispered sighs.
As shadows dance, a melody flows,
In a bewitching world, time slows.

The radiant hues of dusk unfold,
Each secret tale in colors told.
Through forests deep and mountains wide,
In every heart, the magic bides.

A shimmering path of silver bright,
Guides weary souls through the night.
With tender grace, their spirits soar,
In echoes cast forevermore.

Luminescent Treasures of the Shadowed Grove

In shadowed groves, where secrets hide,
Luminescent treasures bide.
Their glow reveals the path unknown,
Where whispers of the forest moan.

Amidst the ferns, the fireflies gleam,
They twinkle like a distant dream.
Each fragile light a candle's spark,
Illuminates the endless dark.

Through ancient trees, the shadows sway,
As twilight summons night from day.
In every rustle, stories loom,
Of magic born in midnight's bloom.

Cloaked in mist, the treasures shine,
Reflecting bits of forgotten time.
In shadowed groves, where echoes thrive,
The pulse of magic comes alive.

Woven Fantasies of Gemstone Light

With every thread of twilight spun,
Woven fantasies begin to run.
In gemstone light, the secrets gleam,
Reflecting hopes and softly dreamed.

Each crystal hue, a tale confined,
In colors bright, the fates aligned.
Through shimmering webs of starry grace,
The heart feels warm in this embrace.

When dawn breaks through the misty veil,
The woven dreams begin to sail.
Upon the winds, they take their flight,
In search of realms adorned with light.

The fantasies of gemstone bright,
Lead weary souls to endless night.
In every glimmer, every spark,
A world awakens from the dark.

Glimmers Beneath the Midnight Canopy

In shadows deep, where fairies play,
The whispers of the night ballet.
Each twinkle tells of ancient lore,
Glimmers spark on enchanted shore.

A silver mist wraps round the trees,
As nightingale sings soft to the breeze.
Starlight dances on the lake,
Each ripple stirs a dream awake.

Moonlit secrets softly sigh,
As dreamers gaze at twilight’s eye.
In every corner, wonders dwell,
Beneath the magic's tender spell.

The owls hoot from their lofty perch,
With solemn eyes, they begin their search.
Mysterious paths invite the bold,
To seek the tales the night has told.

And as the dawn begins to break,
The shadows fade, the dreams we take.
Yet memories of the midnight glow,
In hearts will linger, soft and low.

Enchanted Fragments of Starlit Whispers

Upon the hill where shadows blend,
Starlit whispers gently send,
A melody of dreams untold,
In silver threads of night, unfold.

Each fragment sings of distant lands,
Where time slips through like softened sands.
In every blink, a wish is cast,
Echoes of the future, past.

The moon, a guardian in the sky,
Watches over when night draws nigh.
Its luminescent glow bestows,
A tapestry where magic grows.

With every breeze, the stories soar,
Of ancient tales and endless lore.
In every heart, a spark ignites,
As enchanted fragments grace the nights.

And in the silence, dreams align,
Crafting worlds, both yours and mine.
In starlit whispers, we shall find,
The secrets of the cosmic mind.

Sparkling Secrets in the Moonlit Glade

In a glade where moonlight streams,
Softly through the twilight beams.
Secrets sparkle, rich and bright,
Guiding wanderers of the night.

The flowers sway with gentle grace,
Inviting all to find their place.
Each petal holds a story fair,
Of love and hope, of fragrant air.

The trees, with branches wide and high,
Reach for the outstretched velvet sky.
In their arms, the stars confide,
The hidden paths that dreams decide.

A crystal pond reflects the light,
Each ripple yields a vision bright.
In moonlit glade, the heart can soar,
Where echoes linger forevermore.

With every step, the magic grows,
Through every sigh, the secret flows.
In stillness deep, we come alive,
In moonlit glade, our spirits thrive.

Fractal Dreams of a Celestial Sorceress

In the realm of endless night,
A sorceress weaves stars of light.
Her fractal dreams swirl and twine,
Painting galaxies, bold and divine.

With whispers soft, she stirs the sky,
A dance of cosmos drifting by.
Each twinkle calls, a spark in place,
A glimpse of time, of endless space.

Her wand, a comet on the run,
Crafts realms where starlit rivers run.
In shimmering paths, she leads the way,
To mystical worlds where wishes play.

Through cosmic threads of bright allure,
She weaves the dreams that hearts seek pure.
In fractal patterns, mysteries lay,
Awaiting those who dare to sway.

With every breath, a story spins,
Of wondrous worlds, of fate and whims.
In dreams, we find the stars align,
Forever captured in space and time.

Luminescent Tokens of Forgotten Lore

In the twilight glow of ancient woods,
Whispers of magic stir in the air,
Tokens of time, wrapped in silence,
Glow softly, revealing secrets rare.

Once held by hands of the wise and old,
Fingers tracing runes in the night,
Each pulse a story, each flicker a tale,
Love and loss woven in light.

Beneath the stars, they dance and twine,
Invisible threads spin old memories,
Bearer of dreams and keeper of fate,
Shining bright 'neath the boughs of trees.

Forgotten by many, yet waiting still,
A gentle reminder of what's been lost,
Seek out the tokens, and listen close,
To the echoes of history, at any cost.

For within their glow, a promise lies,
To open the heart and heal the soul,
In luminescent whispers, we'll find our way,
Through the shadows of time, we'll learn to be whole.

Beacons of Light Amongst Dark Spells

When shadows close in, and hope feels thin,
A flicker ignites, brushing the sky,
Beacons of light, steadfast and bright,
Guiding our spirits, they never die.

Through the weave of the night, spells cast in gloom,
These glimmers stand tall, fearless, and true,
Each sparkle a promise of softer days,
When skies will clear, and dreams come anew.

In the depths of despair, or paths filled with fright,
These flames remind us we're never alone,
With courage set forth, our hearts will take flight,
In the glow of the dark, our spirits have grown.

Amidst the chaos, find solace in rays,
That dance and flutter, lighting our way,
For in the unknown, we often must tread,
Beacons of light shall guide us instead.

Let them be anchors when tides pull us deep,
For hope is a magic that helps us to leap,
Into realms where shadows dare not encroach,
Illuminated by love's tender approach.

Celestial Trinkets on a Witch's Altar

Upon the altar, where moonlight spills,
Celestial trinkets lie in array,
Crafted by hands that embrace the night,
Holding the power of magic's sway.

Feathers of starlight, and shells from the sea,
Gathered in silence, touched by the breeze,
Charmed with intentions, both gentle and bold,
Each one a story, a wish on the freeze.

Rings etched with runes that whisper to air,
Glowing with secrets of love and despair,
Potions that bubble, weaving fate in a jar,
Reminders of journeys both near and afar.

Incense that swirls like a dance of delight,
Capturing essence of memories bright,
In the heart of the witch, the cosmos unfolds,
A tapestry woven, with wonders untold.

So gather them 'round in the still of the night,
Celestial trinkets, our guiding light,
In the peace of the moment, we will find our truth,
In the magic of life, we reclaim our youth.

Glints of Enigma in the Witch's Brew

In the cauldron's depths, where mysteries swirl,
Glints of enigma beckon the mind,
Froths of potion, alight with spells,
Secrets submerged, waiting to find.

A pinch of the past, a dash of the now,
Wisdom from elders, taught through the years,
With a flick of the wrist, intent set to flow,
Brewed in the silence, shaped by our fears.

Each bubble a whisper, a thought, or a dream,
Carried on currents, unseen streams,
Infusing the air with heady delight,
As night dances in on ethereal beams.

Glass vials jingle, cradled in twine,
Each containing a wish or a tear,
To sip or to save, a choice to be made,
Within every drop lies the heart of a seer.

So gather 'round closely, dear friends of the night,
For there in the brew, we'll find our own flight,
With glints of enigma, and courage to dare,
In the flames of the witch's art, we will share.

Abundant Treasures of the Night Realm

In shadows deep where secrets hide,
The stars unfold on the dark tide.
Whispers of magic dance through the air,
With every breath, enchantments bare.

The moonlit path, a silver thread,
Guides wandering souls where dreams are fed.
Crickets lull in a soothing song,
As night enfolds, we all belong.

Each glimmering gem, a story captured,
In twilight's arms, the heart is raptured.
Fireflies twinkle, a gentle glow,
Lighting the world in a mystic flow.

Among the trees, the spirits play,
In moonlit realms, they weave their sway.
A tapestry rich with ancient lore,
Awaits the brave, that seek for more.

So listen close to the night's embrace,
Find hidden wonders, a sacred space.
For in the dark, beneath the skies,
Abundant treasures in silence lie.

Radiant Mysteries in Autumn's Grip

As autumn leaves begin to fall,
The world transforms, a golden call.
Crisp air whispers of change and grace,
In nature's heart, a warm embrace.

Each color bursts, a fiery dance,
Inviting all to take a chance.
The harvest moon, a watchful eye,
Sees secrets beneath the fading sky.

With every rustle, tales unfold,
Of whispered dreams and hearts of gold.
The wind, a bard, with stories spun,
Of life reborn beneath the sun.

Beneath the boughs of ancient oak,
The tendrils of time, they softly invoke.
In golden light, the magic swells,
Radiant mysteries, nature tells.

So tread with care on this path anew,
For autumn’s grip holds wonders true.
With each sweet breath of crisp delight,
The world transforms in autumn’s light.

Reflections in Diamonds of Night's Pool

Beneath the stars, a tranquil pond,
Where dreams and shadows linger fond.
A mirror holds the night's embrace,
Reflecting truths in jeweled grace.

In ripples soft, the secrets flow,
Of whispered hopes, the heart's glow.
The moon dips low, a silver kiss,
In nighttime's calm, we find our bliss.

Each twinkling star, a wish bestowed,
In silent waters where tales explode.
The quiet murmurs, the stories shared,
Of souls entwined, of hearts laid bare.

So sit awhile, and listen near,
To the echoing joy, the lingering fear.
For in the depths, the wisps of light,
Reveal reflections in the night.

With every breath, a moment bold,
In diamonds bright, the secrets told.
So seek the peace in twilight's scroll,
For whispers rest in night's deep pool.

The Touch of Enchantment on Woven Branches

In the forest's heart, the branches weave,
A tapestry rich, of dreams to conceive.
Each leaf a whisper, a story spun,
In the soft embrace of the setting sun.

The gentle breeze sings through the trees,
Carrying secrets on the autumn leaves.
With every rustle, beneath the bough,
The touch of enchantment reveals the how.

Fairy lights glimmer in twilight's hold,
A warm embrace from the stories old.
Mystical beings entwined in dance,
Bathe in the warmth of magic's chance.

Amidst the branches, life finds its way,
In shadows and light where dreams sway.
For woven together, both dark and bright,
The touch of enchantment, a radiant light.

So wander deep, let your spirit roam,
In the forest's grip, you'll find your home.
With every step, a magic chance,
To feel the wonder in nature's dance.

Crystalized Moments in Bewitching Darkness

In shadows deep where secrets hide,
A glimmering light begins to glide.
Crystals whisper tales of time,
In darkness bound, their beauty chimes.

Like starlit skies in silent night,
Each fragment holds a fleeting sight.
Moments caught in frozen grace,
In bewitching realms, we find our place.

With every breath, the magic swirls,
Around the veins of ancient worlds.
A tapestry of dreams interlace,
In every heart, a hidden trace.

The echoes sing of paths once trod,
Ensnared in wonders, we feel odd.
Yet crystal shards bring clarity,
In darkness lit with rarity.

So gather round, the ethereal glow,
Embrace the moments as they flow.
For in the night, we're not alone,
In crystalized dreams, we find our home.

Gems Beneath Moonlit Spells

Underneath the crescent moon,
Gems of wonder softly croon.
Each facet sparkles, tales unfurl,
Beneath the glow, our hearts twirl.

With every beam, a promise made,
A treasure hidden, never swayed.
Moonlit spells wrap round like vines,
In gentle winds, the magic twines.

They tell of lovers long since lost,
Of fortunes found that come at cost.
Yet, in their depths, we see the truth,
A glint of sorrow, shade of youth.

Recall the nights when wishes danced,
In shimmering light, our hopes advanced.
For gems that twinkle in the night,
Hold secrets cloaked in pure delight.

So let us gather, hand in hand,
In jeweled worlds where dreams expand.
With moonlit spells to guide our way,
We'll chase the dawn, where shadows play.

Shimmering Whispers of Enchantment

In glades where silence weaves its charm,
Shimmering whispers, sweet and warm.
A breeze that carries tales of yore,
Opens the heart, unlocks the door.

With every rustle, secrets twine,
In nature's cradle, pure, divine.
Enchantments linger in the air,
As if the world itself does care.

Dream-woven tales on petals rest,\nA gentle hymn, a heart's quest.
Golden threads of light cascade,
In shimmering hues, the shadows fade.

Each leaf a story, each stone a song,
In this realm where we belong.
With every pulse, a voice resounds,
Echoing magic that surrounds.

So let us wander, hand in hand,
Through whispered woods, enchanted land.
Where shimmering paths invite our eyes,
To trace the dreams beneath the skies.

Glimmers of the Night's Secrets

In twilight's hush, the secrets creep,
Glimmers dance where shadows weep.
The night unveils its tender guise,
In whispered tones, the magic lies.

Stars like lanterns softly blink,
Inviting minds to pause and think.
Each twinkle holds a hidden lore,
Of time and space, forevermore.

The velvet sky, a satin sheet,
Covers dreams that never meet.
Yet in the dark, a spark ignites,
Illuminating hidden sights.

Embrace the stillness, heed the call,
Of night's soft breath that cradles all.
For in each glimmer, truth entwines,
A tapestry of life's designs.

So venture forth, let shadows guide,
Through glimmers where the heart confides.
In every secret, magic's thread,
We find the paths where we are led.

Portraits of Light in Enchanted Spaces

In shadowed halls where whispers gleam,
The portraits dance with fading dreams.
Their colors bright, a tale to weave,
In every glance, a heart to cleave.

With golden strokes, they hold the past,
A flicker found, too rare to last.
Each canvas breathes, a life anew,
In radiant hues, the moments grew.

Through moonlit veins, the magic flows,
As time unfolds, the beauty glows.
The laughter shared, the tears embraced,
In timeless realms, we seek our place.

A spark ignites where secrets dwell,
In hidden nooks, our stories swell.
Each flicker tells of love and strife,
A glowing thread that weaves our life.

So step into this world of art,
Where shadows leap and light won't part.
For every glance a truth unveils,
In enchanting light, our spirit sails.

The Illumination of Secrets After Dark

When stars emerge, the world transforms,
In velvet skies, the magic warms.
Each gentle flicker whispers low,
Of hidden thoughts we yearn to know.

With shadows deep, the laughter fades,
Revealing dreams in twilight's shades.
The silent corners, secrets keep,
In hushed repose, the mysteries seep.

As lanterns glow in dusky air,
They light the path for hearts that dare.
To chase the phantoms of the night,
And find the truth in soft moonlight.

In secret glades where shadows play,
The stories born at end of day.
They twine and twist, like ivy's grasp,
In every breath, the night'll clasp.

So let the dark become your guide,
And in its depths, new worlds abide.
Hold tight the dreams both wild and stark,
For every soul, a sparkling spark.

Sleight of Hand in the Dust of Dreams

In twilight's grasp where shadows sway,
A trickster's laugh will steal the day.
With deftened hands, the magic spins,
As laughter dances, mischief grins.

Among the stars, the dreams take flight,
In whispered tales of dark and light.
A sleight of hand, both swift and sly,
As dust of dreams begins to fly.

The art of change, a playful scheme,
Where wishes hide in every gleam.
With opening hearts, the secrets shared,
In shadows cast, the world declared.

Yet in this game of sight and sound,
The truth is lost, but magic found.
For every sleight, a heart exposed,
A tapestry of lives composed.

So dance with me through veil and mist,
Embrace the dreams that twist and twist.
In every breath, a story blooms,
In dust of dreams, our spirit looms.

The Allure of Prismatic Murmurs

In gentle hues where spirits glide,
The colors blend, their secrets hide.
Each prism whispers, soft and clear,
Of realms uncharted, wrapped in cheer.

With every glance, a spark ignites,
A flickering dance of starry nights.
In echoes bright, the worlds unite,
As shadows fade in morning light.

A melody of hearts entwined,
In every note a truth defined.
The whispers call, the rhythm plays,
As daydreams weave through endless bays.

So chase the light, embrace the song,
In prismatic paths, we all belong.
For every step in colors grand,
Leads us within a magic land.

So close your eyes and take the flight,
For in these murmurs, there is light.
A glow that holds each hope and sigh,
In prismatic realms where dreams can fly.

Flickers of Enchantment in Still Waters

In the hush where whispers thread,
Ripples dance on dreams unsaid.
Moonlight weaves a silver seam,
Bathed in the glow of a waking dream.

Beneath the waves where secrets sigh,
Fairies flit and fireflies fly.
The water's edge holds tales long spun,
Each flicker a sparkle, each drop a sun.

Lily pads wear crowns of dew,
Echoing moments old yet new.
In quietude, the heart can find,
Enchantments woven, heart and mind.

A breeze will carry a lover's tune,
Under the watchful gaze of the moon.
Every ripple tells a story clear,
Of dreams, of hopes, drawing near.

As stars reflect on surfaces still,
Magic lingers, elusive, a thrill.
In still waters, a tale begins,
Flickers of magic, where hope wins.

Glinting Dreams on a Mystic Path

Upon a path where starlight spills,
Dreams entwine like ivy's frills.
Footsteps dance on leaves of gold,
Tales of wonder silently told.

Misty shadows cradle the night,
Every turn reveals a new light.
Glinting whispers of fate's embrace,
Along the way, the heart finds grace.

Ancient trees with secrets bared,
Guardians of all who dared.
Their gnarled roots hold stories deep,
In their shade, both hope and sleep.

Echoes of laughter float on air,
Carried by dreams with beauty rare.
Onward we wander, led by the stars,
Through glinting dreams and timeless cars.

A tapestry woven of light and dark,
Each thread a dream, a vibrant spark.
Mystic paths where shadows sway,
Lead us on our brightened way.

Stardust and Shadows with a Wizard's Touch

In the depth of a twilight canopy,
Whispers of magic stir quietly.
Stardust twinkles in shadows deep,
Where mysteries within the night creep.

A wand held close, the essence of light,
Looms large against the cloak of night.
Words of power ripple through space,
Each note a spell, a warm embrace.

A cauldron bubbles with visions bright,
Forming dreams in the still of night.
Glimmers of hope in bubbling brew,
Awakening wonders as old as dew.

The dance of shadows in candle glow,
Reveals the secrets the stars bestow.
With every flicker, a legend unfolds,
Stories of old, waiting to be told.

With a wizard’s touch, the world can change,
Transmuting fears, its essence strange.
In stardust and shadows, magic flows,
In whispered spells, the heart surely knows.

Charmed Echoes of Hidden Pearls

In the depths where currents weave,
Charmed echoes of pearls believe.
Glistening in the sun's warm glow,
Treasures of time, the heart will know.

Each whispering wave a song of lore,
Breathing life on the ocean floor.
Hidden dreams, both far and near,
Yearning to surface, pure and clear.

Nautical tales swaying like sails,
Journeying forth on mythical trails.
Shells hold secrets of long-lost grace,
Revealing history in their embrace.

Below the surface, the world awaits,
Life emerging through ancient gates.
With every ebb, a story learned,
In each tide, a longing burned.

Charmed echoes call to forgotten hearts,
Invisible threads strumming arts.
In hidden pearls, life's wonders flow,
A treasure of dreams, waiting to grow.

Moons of Dreaming on the Witch's Isle

On the isle where shadows sway,
Moonlight whispers secrets gay.
Waves of magic paint the shore,
Dreams awaken, spirits soar.

Each night brings a silken veil,
Guiding hearts through eerie tale.
Banshees wail, enchantments cling,
Softly hear the faery sing.

Ancient trees with voices low,
Tell of love, both high and low.
Stars above, a twinkling guide,
In this realm where dreams abide.

Through the mist, the shadows play,
Hiding truths that drift away.
With each step on mossy ground,
Lost in wonder, spellbound found.

With the dawn, the magic fades,
Yet in hearts, the memory wades.
On the isle, the dreams remain,
Echoing in a soft refrain.

Flickering Stars Tempt the Midnight Gales

In the hush, the stars do weave,
Tales of wonders, hearts believe.
Gently flicker, glances cast,
Mysteries from the shadows past.

Chasing whispers through the night,
Ghostly dances, pure delight.
Breath of winter, crisp and bright,
Tempting souls to take their flight.

Moonbeams glow on silent seas,
Carried forth by midnight's breeze.
What will dawn's soft light reveal,
When the dreams begin to heal?

Sprinkled wishes, lost and found,
Through the air, enchantments sound.
Night's embrace, a tender balm,
Holding hands, it feels so calm.

As the stars begin to fade,
All the hopes we dare not trade.
In the waking world we tread,
Carried forth on silver thread.

Enigmas Adorned in Night's Fabric

In the night, enigmas dance,
Spinning tales that hold a chance.
Woven threads of dark and light,
Truths unravel in the night.

Whispers echo 'neath the trees,
Secrets carried on the breeze.
Patterns drawn in starlit air,
Unseen wonders, sweet and rare.

Crimson shadows softly sway,
Guiding wanderers on their way.
In the silence, hearts entwined,
Seeking what the soul can find.

Every glance, a fleeting spark,
Filling voids that haunt the dark.
Echoes beckon from afar,
As we chase each distant star.

In this tapestry of night,
Looming magic, pure delight.
Each enigma leads to more,
Unlocking every hidden door.

Charmed Souls Beneath the Hidden Glades

In the glades where shadows blend,
Charmed souls gather, hearts will mend.
Nature hums a soothing tune,
Underneath the watchful moon.

Whispers linger in the air,
Woven stories everywhere.
Beneath the boughs, the laughter glows,
Bringing life to all that grows.

Lights like fireflies softly gleam,
Painting dreams in twilight's dream.
Each step taken, magic found,
As the spirits dance around.

In this realm where hearts unite,
Friendship bonds shine pure and bright.
Holding hands, eternally,
Lost in bliss, wild and free.

As the dawn begins to break,
All the dreams we dare to make.
In the glades our souls will play,
Charmed together, come what may.

Glistening Visions from the Fae's Delight

In the glade where shadows dance,
Fae whispers twirl in moon's soft glance.
Petals shimmer, secrets weave,
Magic lingers, hearts believe.

Glimmers spark where dreams take flight,
A waltz of wonder through the night.
With every laugh, a spell is cast,
In this realm where joy is vast.

Silver streams of starlit beams,
Cradle hopes and shimmered dreams.
Brush of wings, a fleeting sight,
Lost in wonders, hearts ignite.

Echoes of a timeless song,
In the woods where night is strong.
Moonlit paths through emerald trees,
Invite the soul to dance with ease.

Whispers sweet, a gentle breeze,
Twinkling lights among the leaves.
Glistening visions twine and sway,
In the Fae's delight, we play.

Mystical Glances of Twilight's Adornment

Twilight spreads her shivering cloak,
A tapestry of whispers spoke.
Colors swirl in fading light,
Mystical glances steal the night.

Beneath the stars, the shadows grow,
Painting secrets in the glow.
With every sigh, the evening sighs,
Underneath the vast, wide skies.

Twinkling gems of evening dew,
Cradle hopes both old and new.
Dreams entwined in twilight's breath,
Charm the heart to dance with death.

As the world begins to rest,
Night's caress, a soothing vest.
Glimmering paths of silver light,
Lead us onward, ever bright.

In this hour where magic sways,
A song of stars, a haunting phrase.
Mystical glances, soft reveal,
In the twilight, truths conceal.

Shattered Moonlight on an Ancient Broom

Shattered moonlight spills like gold,
Brushing stories yet untold.
The ancient broom begins to stir,
Whispers weave in every purr.

Dust of ages clings like mist,
Every bristle holds a tryst.
With gentle sweep, the past unfolds,
Timeless echoes, brave and bold.

Floating softly through the night,
Carving paths of pale moonlight.
Each flicker tells of dreams once lost,
Awakening, no matter the cost.

In the hush of midnight's grace,
Ancient secrets leave no trace.
Swirling leaves on gravel roads,
The broom remembers what erodes.

Shattered moonbeams guide the way,
Inviting all who dare to stay.
Once again the magic blooms,
On the hearts of those with dreams.

Flickering Insights of Midnight Splendor

Flickering lights in shadows play,
Casting dreams that fade away.
Midnight whispers soft and low,
Invite the heart to feel the glow.

In the hush, a gentle sigh,
Living moments that drift by.
Every spark a fleeting chance,
To step into a mystic dance.

Glimmering truths in starlit pools,
Charming minds, enchanting fools.
Veils of night, so rich and deep,
Guard the dreams that we shall keep.

Insights twine in silver threads,
Binding whispers where hope spreads.
As the world fades into dusk,
Embrace the night, ignite the trust.

Flickering visions, soft, divine,
Entwine our fates, your hand in mine.
Midnight splendor calls us near,
In the quiet, love draws near.

Hues of Magic in a Twilight Breeze

In the twilight air, colors align,
Whispers of magic, soft and divine.
Shadows dance lightly, secrets unfold,
Painting the dusk in stories untold.

Stars flicker gently, a mystical rhyme,
Catching the dreams that slip through time.
Each hue a spell, each shade a thought,
In the canvas of night, enchantments are wrought.

The breeze carries laughter, a tune from afar,
Guiding the heart where wonders are.
Mysteries flourish in the lavender glow,
As the world spins quietly, wrapped in a bow.

Cloaks of evening brush over the ground,
Crickets are choristers, a symphonic sound.
With each breath, magic glimmers and sways,
A tapestry woven in twilight's soft blaze.

In the heart of the night, hope dares to soar,
Painting the darkness with tales of yore.
In every shadow, in every breeze,
Lies the essence of dreams, a soul’s gentle tease.

Luminous Secrets Amongst the Thorns

Amidst the thicket, secrets are spun,
Glimmers of wisdom in shadows run.
Thorns may be fierce, but beauty remains,
In the half-light where enchantment gains.

Each petal whispers, each leaf a song,
In the heart of the wild, where souls belong.
Luminous fireflies dance through the dark,
Illuminating pathways where dreams leave a mark.

Fingers of light stretch through tangled vines,
Drawing forth tales where the ancient aligns.
Every thorn holds a story untold,
Of lovers and legends, of brave and of bold.

In the silence of night, the magic is spread,
A silken web woven, dreams delicately fed.
For those who are brave, and venture inside,
Lies a world of wonders, where secrets confide.

With courage, they carry their hearts like a torch,
Embracing the thorns where dreams they will scorch.
Amongst the wild whispers of roots and of stones,
They find luminous truths, beyond the mere bones.

The Witch's Treasures Under a Starry Veil

Beneath the vast night, treasures lie deep,
Hidden in shadows where secrets keep.
A witch's allure, all wrapped in a spell,
Veiled by the stars, where enchantments dwell.

Pots brimming with potions, each hue a delight,
Glistening softly in the luminous night.
Crystals, they shimmer, whispering lore,
Of ancient enchantments and legends of yore.

In her cauldron, the moonlight is stirred,
Casting reflections, each wish is heard.
The scent of wild herbs fills the cool air,
As magic ignites in the stillness, rare.

Echoes of laughter, a mischievous sound,
Float through the night, like wishes unbound.
With wands made of willow and hearts full of fire,
They call on the stars, their hopes rising higher.

Under the starlight, her power takes flight,
A dance of the shadows, alive in the night.
With each twinkling star, the treasures reveal,
The mysteries woven under magic's soft seal.

Fragments of Light in Darkened Woods

In the heart of the woods, where shadows entwine,
Fragments of light, like dreams, brightly shine.
Through the dense thickets, secrets are thrown,
Whispers of longings in twilight's soft tone.

Each leaf a story, each branch a sigh,
Glimmers of hope, they catch the eye.
Moonbeams fall gently on paths overgrown,
Leading the wanderer far from the known.

Flickering lanterns dance in the shade,
Revealing the magic where fears are laid.
With every soft step, the heart starts to leap,
Guided by dreams that the dark woods keep.

In the crisp silence, the magic takes hold,
Whispers of starlight, both brave and bold.
In the rustling leaves, adventures await,
For those who believe in a luminous fate.

So venture forth into nature's embrace,
Where fragments of light leave a silvery trace.
In the darkened woods, where wonder resides,
Fear not the shadows, let courage be your guide.

Glorious Ribbons in a Weaver’s Hands

In a twilight glow, ribbons sway,
Colors merging, dance and play.
A tapestry of dreams unfurled,
Weaver's magic, stitching worlds.

Threads of laughter, sorrow's hue,
Each entwined with tales anew.
With deft hands, she guides each strand,
Crafting destinies, mapped and planned.

Whispers breeze through fibers bright,
Stories woven, day to night.
In every twist, a secret hides,
A life envisioned, love abides.

Patterns hidden in the weave,
Tell the stories we believe.
With every knot, a heartbeat sings,
The legacy of all our things.

So marvel at her skillful art,
For in each ribbon lies a heart.
In colors bold, she finds her peace,
A weaver's grace that will not cease.

Iridescence Dancing on the Wind

Through emerald fields, a shimmer flies,
A dance of light beneath the skies.
Each flit and flutter, whispers sweet,
Ethereal beings, none can defeat.

Wings adorned in hues divine,
Glinting sparks of the sun's design.
They sway like wishes on a breeze,
In nature's song, their hearts appease.

Each moment sparkles, fleeting fast,
Elusive shadows, seldom last.
Yet joy in every fleeting glimpse,
A fleeting bond that softly primps.

Casting rainbows as they glide,
Dreamlike visions, side by side.
They carry hopes on gentle waves,
In every heart, their magic saves.

So close your eyes and feel the air,
Let iridescence lift your care.
Allow the dance of peace to soar,
On beams of light, forevermore.

Wands of Wonder at Day's End

As daylight wanes, the wands ignite,
Casting spells in the twilight.
Whispers linger, soft and low,
Magic flows where shadows grow.

With every flick, the stars align,
In perfect rhythm, pure divine.
From ancient wood, their power glows,
Creating worlds that no one knows.

In silver mist, intentions rise,
Chasing dreams across the skies.
With hearts ablaze, they conjure light,
Transforming darkness into bright.

Each wand holds secrets, age-old tales,
Of mighty quests and whispered gales.
They spark a journey, grand and bold,
In every flick, a heart of gold.

So let the magic weave its thread,
As night unfolds and dreams are fed.
For wands of wonder, sturdy and grand,
Guide our spirits, hand in hand.

Threads of Fate in Glinting Time

In twilight's hush, the threads unwind,
Stitching tales of hearts entwined.
Glimmers spark in shadow's grasp,
Moments cherished, tight we clasp.

Time's tapestry, a vibrant weave,
Holds the stories we believe.
With every year, a cycle spins,
In threads of fate, our journey begins.

Through laughter, tears, the motifs blend,
Lives interwoven, joys extend.
Each golden strand a memory kept,
In whispered dreams, our futures leapt.

A loom of stars in midnight's glow,
Crafts the paths we long to know.
Each thread glistens, destiny calls,
In the fabric of life, our spirits enthrall.

So cherish the tapestry we find,
For in each thread, the heart is blind.
Dance in the rhythm of time's embrace,
In threads of fate, we find our place.

Brilliant Hues in the Enshrouded Wilds

In shadowed groves where whispers cling,
Bright colors dance on nature's wing.
Emerald leaves and sapphire skies,
Soft murmurs rise as daylight dies.

Glints of gold through branches peek,
Where nimble creatures nod and speak.
A tapestry of dreams unfolds,
In every thread, a tale retold.

Crimson blooms in twilight's grace,
Florals twirl in a delicate chase.
Moonlit nectar, sweetly caught,
In this wild realm of wonder sought.

Flickering lights like distant stars,
Chasing shadows, shifting bars.
Enchanting sights in fleeting chance,
Lead the heart into a dance.

Amidst the hush, a secret hum,
Nature’s heart, a steady drum.
In enshrouded wilds, vibrant and true,
Life awakens in brilliant hues.

Glittering Visions in the Witching Hour

Beneath the moon's ethereal glow,
Visions waltz in silken flow.
Whispers weave through the midnight air,
Casting spells, a timeless snare.

Twinkling stars like scattered dreams,
Glittering softly, or so it seems.
With every breath, a story spins,
Of ancient magic and quiet sins.

The clock strikes twelve—a moment's sigh,
As shadows dance and spirits fly.
Echoes of laughter brush the night,
Painting the dark with twinkling light.

In this hour when dreams collide,
Secrets bloom, and fears abide.
Hearts align in a cosmic thread,
Where past and future gently tread.

So listen close, and you may find,
A spark of wonder, fate entwined.
In glittering visions, brave and bold,
The witching hour's tales unfold.

Enigma in the Radiance of the Spellbound

In twilight's breath, an enigma glows,
Where magic twirls and time slows.
Mysteries wrapped in starlit lace,
Whispered secrets in every space.

Radiance blossoms, a soft embrace,
Awakening wonders in hidden place.
Each shadow breathes a tale obscure,
Of love and loss, of hearts unsure.

The air is thick with unseen threads,
Crafted whims, where the story spreads.
Step with caution, or take the leap,
Into dreams where the wild things creep.

Glimmers reflect on the misty lake,
Every ripple, a choice to make.
Hold tight the magic, let it unfold,
In the radiant night, be brave and bold.

With every heartbeat, the mystery calls,
Through winding paths and ancient walls.
In the glow of wonders, profound and sound,
Find your heart in the spellbound ground.

Radiant Shadows Under the Sorceress's Watch

In depth of night, where shadows play,
Radiance weaves and drifts away.
Beneath the stars, a whisper's guide,
Under the sorceress's watchful stride.

Glimmers dance on the edges of sight,
A tapestry spun from darkness and light.
Each flicker tells of ages past,
Of magic’s hold, of fates amassed.

Espressos of dreams blend with the night,
In every heart lays a flickering light.
Echoes linger, soft and low,
As shadows shift in a somber flow.

Woven spells in the rustling leaves,
Mystical whispers through twilight weaves.
With every heartbeat, tale and wish,
Conjured into the evening's dish.

So heed the call where shadows sway,
In radiant shapes, let your heart play.
Under the sorceress, find your path,
In these luminous trails reside the aftermath.

Dazzling Reflections in the Mystic Pool

In the depths of water, secrets gleam,
Whispers of wisdom, so rare they seem.
Ripples dance lightly, a silvery sheen,
Mirrors of magic where wishes convene.

Flickering candles in the twilight glow,
Casting soft shadows on dreams like snow.
Stars above shimmer, in their gentle grace,
Guiding lost travelers to a bright place.

Moonlight gathers, a veil of delight,
Kissing the surface with ethereal light.
In this still haven, the world feels new,
Each droplet reflects a heart's hidden view.

Mystic creatures, both wise and bold,
Share tales of old, in whispers told.
Beneath the surface, the stories unfold,
Of heroes and legends, bright glimmers of gold.

So linger a moment, let your heart speak,
In the mystic pool where the calm hearts seek.
For in its embrace, you'll find your own song,
A universe waiting, where you belong.

Fragments of Dawn at the Sorceress's Feet

When dawn breaks softly, painting the sky,
With hues of peach and whispers of sigh.
The sorceress stands, wise, aglow,
Sharing the secrets that only winds know.

Each fragment of sunlight, a glimmering grace,
Flicks through the shadows, a warm embrace.
Patterns of magic weave through the air,
Invoking the power of dreams laid bare.

Her laughter a melody, light as a breeze,
In the heart of the moment, the world aims to please.
She dances with starlight, wraps night in a quilt,
Mending the wounds of the dreams that we built.

With every heartbeat, the earth comes alive,
As fragments of hope begin to revive.
In enchanted circles, the spirits awake,
Welcoming dawn with each move that they make.

So bow to the sorceress, humble and meek,
For wisdom flows deeply, unwavering, unique.
In the dawn's bright glow, let your spirit take flight,
In fragments of time, embrace endless light.

Ethereal Crystals in the Starlit Fog

Beneath the blanket of shimmering night,
Crystals dance gently, catching the light.
In the starlit fog, they scatter and gleam,
Creating a tapestry woven from dreams.

Each glimmer a promise, a wish set adrift,
Stories entangled in a celestial gift.
Echoes of laughter float high in the air,
As magic sparkles, weaving joy everywhere.

In shadows that twinkle, a soft giggle hides,
Unseen by the world, where enchantment abides.
Ethereal whispers glide on the breeze,
Like secrets exchanged between gnarled old trees.

As the night deepens, the crystals ignite,
Illumined reflections, a dance of pure light.
They shatter the silence with a shimmering song,
Each note a reminder that we all belong.

So wander these moments, lost in their glow,
Where mysteries linger and dreams freely flow.
In ethereal crystals, the night will inspire,
A realm of reflections where hearts can conspire.

Shimmering Whispers Through the Forest Veil

Through the forest veil, secrets entwined,
Shimmering whispers of magic confined.
The green canopy sways with the breeze,
Holding the stories of ancient trees.

Moonbeams descend like silver lace threads,
Guiding lost travelers on paths that they tread.
Each leaf a messenger, soft tales it bears,
Of creatures that dwell in enchanted lairs.

Moss carpets soft underfoot, a gentle breath,
As shadows play games, teasing life and death.
In the heart of the night, the forest unfolds,
Revealing the secrets the wildness holds.

From thickets and thorns, the nightingale sings,
Notes like enchantments on delicate wings.
A symphony woven through branches and bark,
With echoes of laughter that bloom in the dark.

So listen closely, when silence is near,
For magic resides in both hope and fear.
Through shimmering whispers, the forest will tell,
The dreams woven gently through its lush, leafy shell.

Potions of Light in the Witch's Grimoire

In a bottle of glass, a shimmer resides,
A flicker of hope that in darkness abides.
Whispers of magic in colors that gleam,
Each sip a spell, each draught a dream.

Through the cauldron's dance, the essence will flow,
Conjuring warmth as the cold winds blow.
With herbs from the forest, and moonlit dew,
A potion of kindness, a heart made anew.

Glimmering shards of the star-laden sky,
Forming elixirs, making spirits fly.
In parchment and ink, the secrets are penned,
A legacy forged, as old foes transcend.

With laughter and light, the brew starts to grow,
An essence of joy that the heart cannot slow.
A dash of adventure, a sprinkle of grace,
In this grimoire's depths, a warm, safe embrace.

So gather the light, in sorrow take flight,
For potions of love will guide you through night.
In the witch's great tome, let your journey ignite,
For within all its pages, the world feels just right.

Ethereal Ornaments in the Moon's Embrace

Under moon's silver sheen, the shadows do gleam,
Adorned with pure magic, like a delicate dream.
Jewels of starlight woven in thread,
Sparkle with whispers of those long since dead.

Garlands of flowers that shimmer and sway,
Dance gently in the soft night’s ballet.
Crafted with care, in twilight's embrace,
Ornaments twinkle with a mystical grace.

Each whispering breeze holds a timeless refrain,
Carried on winds that once knew her name.
Cascades of luminescence lace the night sky,
In the moon's gentle glow, the lost dreams still fly.

Shimmering crystals, they glisten and glow,
Like memories cherished that never will slow.
Ethereal treasures in shadows concealed,
In moonlight unveiled, all secrets revealed.

Beneath silver arches where wishes take flight,
Dreamers entwined in the soft velvet night.
With each twinkling star, a new story begins,
An ornament clasping the magic within.

Frosted Facets of Midnight Magic

In the hush of the night, when the stars come to play,
Frosted facets twinkle, where shadows lay.
Crystals of silence, adorned in a glow,
Guarding the secrets that only night knows.

With whispers of frost on the edges of dreams,
A tapestry woven with shimmer and beams.
Each flake tells a story, both tender and bold,
Of moments in twilight that shimmer like gold.

Invitations of starlight beckon the brave,
To dance with the shadows, the magic to crave.
In this midnight realm, lost wishes take flight,
As glimmers of dreams ignite in the night.

Through landscapes enchanted with ice and with fire,
Waltzes of wonders rekindle desire.
A spellbinding chill that ignites the heart's flame,
In the frost of the night, we find warmth in the name.

So gather the sparkles that whisper and shout,
Celebrate the beauty of what life's about.
In enchanted frost, let our spirits take wing,
For in every facet, a new magic springs.

Whims of the Night in Crystal Waters

By the edge of the lake, where the shadows do creep,
Whims of the night dance, while the world is asleep.
Crystal waters shimmer with secrets untold,
Where laughter echoes and mysteries unfold.

Dewdrops like diamonds adorn every leaf,
Weaving tales of the night, both joyful and brief.
Each ripple a whisper from the depths of the sea,
Calling the lost ones to come and set free.

The night wraps its arms in a silken embrace,
Beneath velvet skies, all time finds its place.
Floating like dreams, the moonlight cascades,
Enchanting the heart, where bravery fades.

In reflections of water, the stars find their dance,
Twilight's sweet magic gives hope a new chance.
With every soft sigh, the heart starts to sway,
With whims of the night leading souls on their way.

So venture to shores where the night spirits dwell,
In crystal waters, let your secrets swell.
For in the night's whispers, the heart learns to yearn,
In the depths of the dark, every soul's chance to turn.

Celestial Glimmers on the Witch's Path

Underneath the whispering trees,
Moonlight dances on the leaves,
Casting shadows, soft and sweet,
Guiding steps with gentle ease.

A flicker in the twilight glow,
Secrets held in silken threads,
Witches roam where night winds blow,
Charting realms where magic spreads.

Stars awaken in the deep,
Echoes of a mystic sigh,
Promises the dreams will keep,
As the night begins to fly.

Potions brewed with ancient lore,
Crystals twinkling, spirits dance,
Little spells to open doors,
In the moonlit, soft romance.

Each step whispers tales of yore,
On the path where shadows gleam,
Celestial glimmers evermore,
Lighting up a witch's dream.

Luminous Threads in the Tapestry of Night

Woven bright 'neath starlit skies,
Luminous threads in twilight weave,
A tapestry where magic lies,
In shadows that the night conceive.

Flickering lights from faraway,
Calling forth the bold and brave,
Whispers of forgotten play,
In the peace that darkness gave.

Crickets sing a serenade,
Embers crackle, softly glow,
In the hush, enchantments laid,
On paths where dreams begin to flow.

Witches gather, cloaked in night,
Casting spells with fleeting grace,
Luminous beams of silver light,
Tracing patterns in time's embrace.

As dawn approaches, spirits soar,
Each thread glimmers, lost in flight,
In the heart of evermore,
Lives the magic of the night.

Twinkling Gems in the Enchanted Wood

In a glen where shadows gleam,
Twinkling gems adorn the floor,
Hidden deep beneath the dream,
Whispers beckon from the core.

Ferns unfurl in emerald pride,
Crimson berries brightly shine,
Elves and fairies, side by side,
Guard their treasures, rare and fine.

Each footfall stirs the silent air,
A melody, soft and clear,
Finding magic lingers there,
In every laugh and every tear.

Underneath the ancient boughs,
Mystical echoes softly sing,
Nature's wonder gently bows,
Inviting all to feel their wing.

As the twilight paints the glade,
Twinkling gems begin to glow,
In the silence, magic made,
In the enchanted wood we know.

Sorcery Sparkles Beneath the Silver Glow

Beneath the silver glow of night,
Sorcery sparkles, wild and free,
Casting dreams in vivid flight,
Weaving tales of mystery.

With each whisper of the breeze,
Magic flows like gentle streams,
Awakening the ancient trees,
In a dance of midnight dreams.

Moonlit paths where shadows sway,
Enchantments twirl like leaves in fall,
Secrets hidden, kept at bay,
Await the brave who heed the call.

Fairy lights in gentle rain,
Kiss the flowers where they bloom,
In their glow, there’s no more pain,
Only whispers in the gloom.

With each spell cast in delight,
The world transforms, a realm anew,
Sorcery sparkles, pure as light,
In the wonders of the brew.

www.ingramcontent.com/pod-product-compliance
Ingram Content Group UK Ltd.
Pitfield, Milton Keynes, MK11 3LW, UK
UKHW021330280125
4330UKWH00005B/467

9 781805 626022